Gone Forever!
Seismosaurus

Rupert Matthews

Heinemann Library
Chicago, Illinois

Customer Service 888-454-2279
Visit our website at www.heinemannlibrary.com

Produced for Heinemann Library by White-Thomson Publishing Ltd.
Edited by Kay Barnham
Book design by John Jamieson
Concept design by Ron Kamen and Paul Davies & Associates
Illustrations by James Field (SGA)
Originated by Que-Net Media™
Printed and bound in China by South China Printing Company

08 07 06 05 04
10 9 8 7 6 5 4 3 2 1

Library of Congress Cataloging-in-Publication Data
Matthews, Rupert.
  Seismosaurus / Rupert Matthews.
     p. cm. -- (Gone forever!)
Summary: Discusses the dinosaur Seismosaurus, including its known physical characteristics, behavior, habitat, and what other creatures were contemporaneous with it, as well as how scientists study fossils and evaluate geological features to learn about extinct organisms.
Includes bibliographical references and index.
  ISBN 1-4034-4912-0 (hardcover) -- ISBN 1-4034-4919-8 (pbk.)
  1. Seismosaurus--Juvenile literature. [1. Seismosaurus. 2. Dinosaurs.] I. Title.
  QE862.S3M33253 2004
  567.913--dc22

                       2003016684

Acknowledgments
The author and publisher are grateful to the following for permission to reproduce copyright material:
Cover photograph reproduced with permission of the Natural History Museum, London.
pp. 4, 20 James L. Amos/Corbis; p. 6 Tom Bean/Corbis; pp. 8, 14 Sinclair Stammers/Science Photo Library; p. 10 Paleontological Museum in Munich; pp. 12, 16, 18, 22 Natural History Museum, London; p. 24 GeoScience; p. 26 Popperfoto.com.

Special thanks to Dr. Peter Makovicky of the Chicago Field Museum for his review of this book.

Every effort has been made to contact copyright holders of any material reproduced in this book. Any omissions will be rectified in subsequent printings if notice is given to the publisher.

Some words are shown in bold, **like this.** You can find out what they mean by looking in the glossary.

Contents

Gone Forever!

Many animals that lived long ago are **extinct.** Although these creatures have disappeared from Earth forever, their **fossils** remained buried in rocks. These fossils show scientists what the extinct animals were like when they were alive.

fish fossil

Seismosaurus was a type of **dinosaur** that lived about 140 million years ago. It is now extinct. Seismosaurus fossils show that this dinosaur was one of the largest animals ever to walk on Earth.

Seismosaurus' Home

Scientists called **paleontologists** have found Seismosaurus **fossils** in North America. The rocks in which the fossils were found can tell us what the land was like when Seismosaurus was alive.

Seismosaurus lived in large, open spaces with gentle hills and wide valleys. The weather was usually warm and fairly wet. This meant that there were plenty of green plants.

Seismosaurus

Stegosaurus

Plants and Trees

Fossils show scientists that low plants, such as **ferns,** covered the ground. There were many different types of fern. Some were short, like those that grow today, while others were much larger.

leaf fossil

8

Fir trees grew in clumps among the ferns,
and taller plants were dotted all around.
Many plants were quite different from those
we see today. These plants are now **extinct.**

9

Pterosaurs

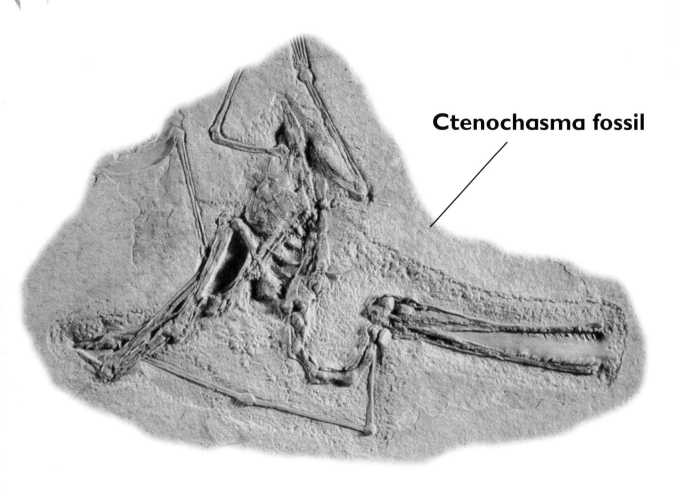

Ctenochasma fossil

Many kinds of flying **reptiles** lived on
Earth at the same time as Seismosaurus.
These creatures are known as
pterosaurs. They are all now **extinct.**

One type of pterosaur was **Ctenochasma.** It had narrow, pointed jaws filled with dozens of long, thin teeth. Ctenochasma fed by scooping up water in its mouth. The water ran between the teeth, leaving small fish and shellfish behind to be eaten.

11

What Was Seismosaurus?

The **fossils** of Seismosaurus show today's **paleontologists** that this was one of the biggest **dinosaurs** ever.

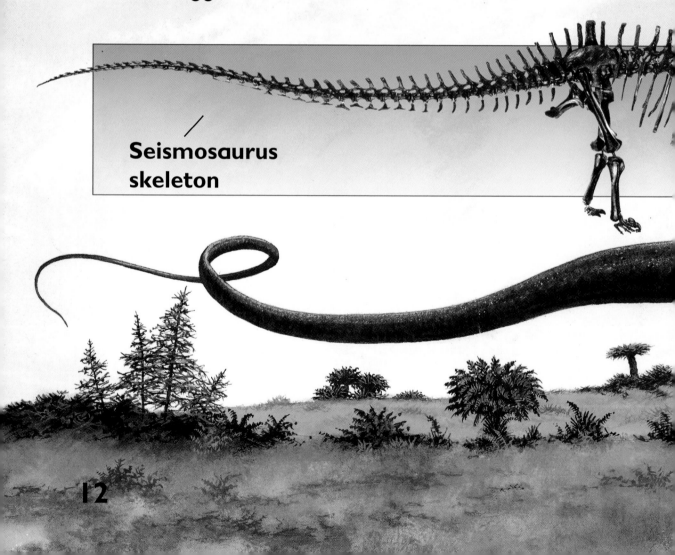

Seismosaurus
skeleton

It was almost half as long as a football field and weighed as much as ten elephants! Seismosaurus was a plant-eater with a very long neck and even longer tail. It walked on all four legs. Because of its size and weight, Seismosaurus probably moved slowly.

Baby Seismosaurus

dinosaur egg fossils

Seismosaurus laid eggs rather than giving birth to live young. The eggs may have been placed in nests dug in soft earth. They were probably buried to keep them safe.

14

After the young **dinosaurs hatched,** they lived together in small groups. The young Seismosaurus ate huge amounts of plants and grew quickly. After one year, the young dinosaurs may have weighed over ten times as much as when they hatched.

Grabbing Food

Seismosaurus had a small mouth, but it was packed with long teeth. These show **paleontologists** what kind of food the **dinosaur** ate and how it ate.

Seismosaurus
skull fossil

Seismosaurus grabbed a mouthful of
leaves and twigs. It then jerked its head
back to snap the food off the tree or bush.

17

Harming Forests

Scientists have found the **fossils** of **cycads.** These were plants that Seismosaurus might have eaten. Tasty, juicy young leaves grew on top of cycad **cones,** which were protected by sharp thorns and tough leaves.

cycad cone fossils

cycad cones

Seismosaurus may have pushed the tall cycad
over to reach its leaves. However, by pushing
over cycads and other trees, Seismosaurus
might have stopped forests from growing.

The Great Rumble

gastrolith fossils

tail

Scientists have found stones among Seismosaurus **fossils.** The **dinosaur** swallowed these stones and kept them in its **crop.** This was a small pouch where food was stored until it was **digested.** The stones are known as **gastroliths.**

20

Seismosaurus did not chew its food. Inside the dinosaur's crop, leaves and twigs were pounded by gastroliths until they became a soft paste. This probably made a loud rumbling sound. Food then passed into the **stomach,** through the **intestines,** and then out of the dinosaur.

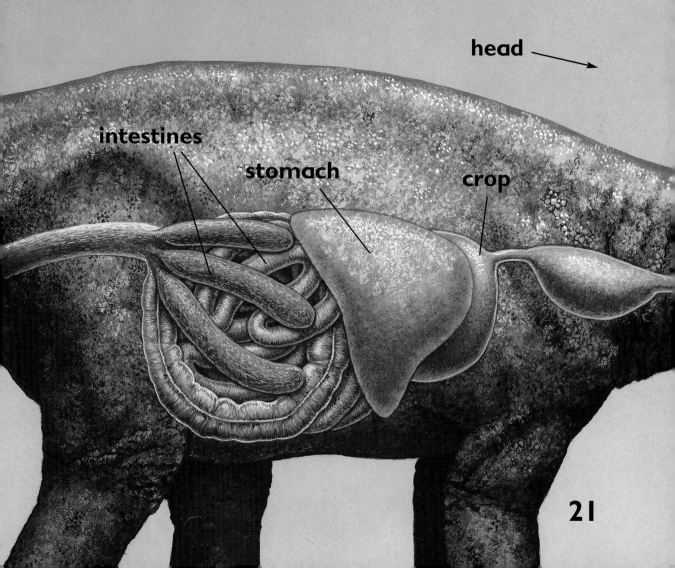

head

intestines

stomach

crop

Dinosaur Dung

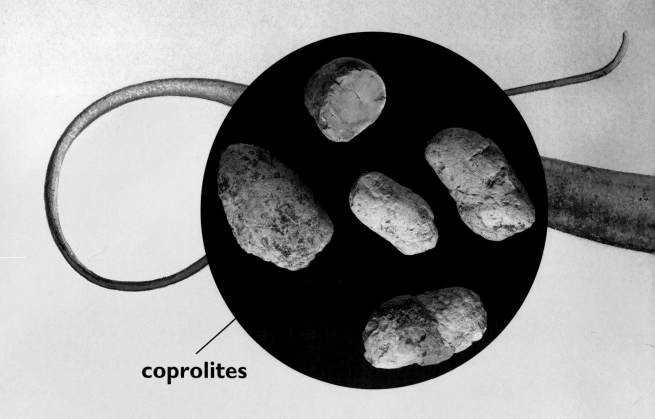

coprolites

Paleontologists have found **fossils** that contain hundreds of pieces of broken twigs, leaves, and tree bark. These are known as **coprolites.** They are the fossils of **dinosaur dung.**

Seismosaurus ate and **digested** an enormous amount of food every day. Afterward, the waste bits of plant were left behind as dung. Some piles of Seismosaurus dung might have been taller than you!

dung

Living with Seismosaurus

The **fossils** of many other types of **dinosaurs** have been found in rocks from the time of Seismosaurus. Many of the dinosaurs were plant-eaters. One of these was **Stegosaurus.**

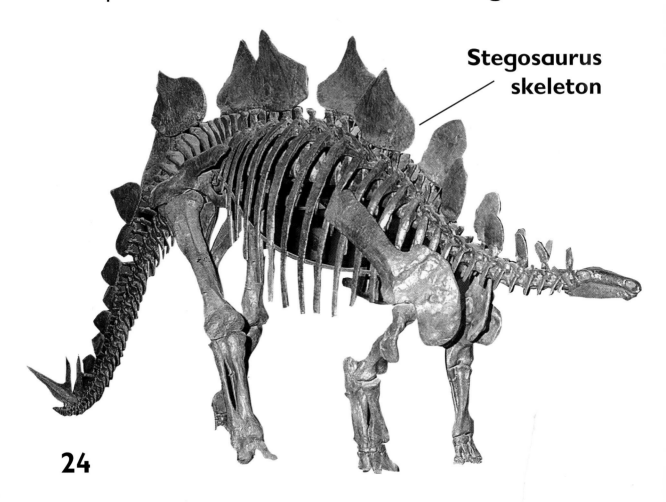

**Stegosaurus
skeleton**

Stegosaurus

Stegosaurus and Seismosaurus were able to live together because they ate different kinds of plants. Stegosaurus had short legs and a short neck. It could only reach plants that grew close to the ground. Seismosaurus ate the taller plants.

Protecting Their Own

fossil dinosaur footprints

Fossil footprints of **dinosaurs** like Seismosaurus tell us that they lived together in **herds.** Larger animals walked at the outer edge of the group. They may have protected the smaller animals.

Allosaurus was a hunter that tried to eat smaller or younger dinosaurs. Scientists think that the larger Seismosaurus may have fought with Allosaurus and chased it away.

Allosaurus

Where Did Seismosaurus Live?

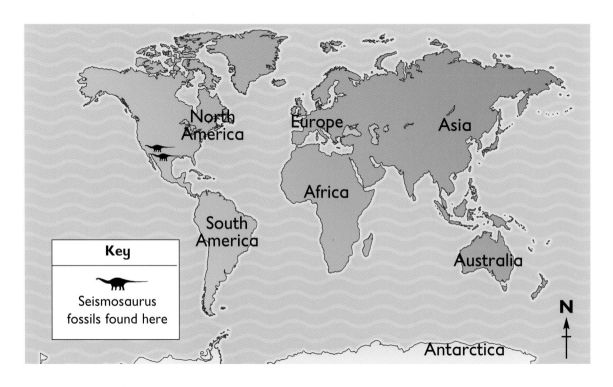

Seismosaurus **fossils** have been found in southwestern parts of North America. Other **dinosaurs,** such as Mamenchisaurus, which looked similar to Seismosaurus, have been found in Europe, Africa, and Asia.

When Did Seismosaurus Live?

Seismosaurus lived between 150 and 133 million years ago. This means that it lived at the end of the Jurassic period, which was in the middle of the Age of the Dinosaurs. The Age of the Dinosaurs is also known as the Mesozoic era.

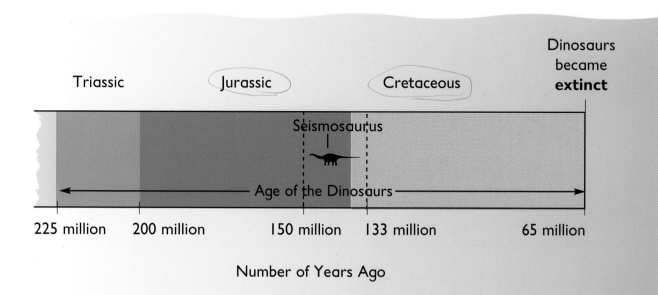

Triassic   Jurassic   Cretaceous   Dinosaurs became **extinct**

Seismosaurus

← Age of the Dinosaurs →

225 million   200 million   150 million   133 million   65 million

Number of Years Ago

29

Fact File

Seismosaurus	
Length:	up to 164 feet (50 meters)
Height:	up to 26 feet (8 meters)
Weight:	up to 33 tons (30 metric tons)
Time:	Late Jurassic period, about 150 to 133 million years ago
Place:	North America

How to Say It

Allosaurus—al-o-sawr-us

Cretaceous—kreh-tay-shus

Ctenochasma—teh-no-kaz-mah

cycad—sy-kad

dinosaur—dine-o-sawr

Diplodocus—di-plod-o-kus

Jurassic—jer-as-ik

Mamenchisaurus— mah-men-key-sawr-us

Mesozoic—meh-so-zo-ik

paleontologist—pay-lee-on-tah-lo-jist

Pterosaur—ter-o-sawr

Seismosaurus—size-mo-sawr-us

Stegosaurus—steg-o-sawr-us

Glossary

Allosaurus large meat-eating dinosaur

cone scaly fruit of certain trees

coprolite piece of animal dung that has become a fossil

crop pouch just above the stomach of some animals in which food is stored for a while

Ctenochasma type of pterosaur, or flying reptile

cycad type of plant that grows fresh leaves at the top of its stem each year

digested describes food that has been broken down in the stomach in order to give the body energy

dinosaur reptile that lived on Earth between 228 and 65 million years ago but has died out

dung waste parts of food that leave the body

extinct once lived on Earth but has died out

fern green plant with large, feathery leaves and no flowers

fir tree with flat, needle-shaped leaves that stay green all year

fossil remains of a plant or animal, usually found in rocks

gastrolith stone kept in an animal's crop to help it digest food

hatch break out of an egg

herd group of animals that live together

intestines part of the body through which food travels once it has been in the stomach

paleontologist scientist who studies the fossils of animals or plants that have died out

pterosaur flying reptile that has died out

reptile cold-blooded animal, such as a snake or lizard

Stegosaurus plant-eating dinosaur

stomach place in the middle of the body where food goes when it is eaten

More Books to Read

Dahl, Michael. *Dinosaur World*. Minneapolis, Minn.: Picture Window Books, 2003.

Kalman, Bobbie. *What Is a Dinosaur?* New York: Crabtree, 1999.

Scott, Janine. *Discovering Dinosaurs*. Minneapolis, Minn.: Compass Point, 2002.

Index